Canned Fruit Syrups

By:

Pamela K. Ritter

© September 2015

# Table of Contents:

Lemon Syrup

Lemon Blueberry Syrup

Mint Syrup

Orange Syrup

Orange Vanilla Syrup

Peach Syrup

Peach Basil Syrup

Peach Vanilla Syrup

Pear Vanilla Maple Syrup

Pineapple Syrup

Pineapple Rum Ginger Syrup

Plum Syrup

Plum Maple Vanilla Syrup

Raspberry Syrup

Raspberry Blackberry Maple Vanilla Syrup

Raspberry Mint Syrup

Raspberry Jalapeno Syrup

Rhubarb Ginger Syrup

Spiced Cherry Syrup

Strawberry Syrup

Strawberry Balsamic Syrup

Strawberry Rhubarb Syrup

Strawberry Vanilla Peppercorn Syrup

Shaved Ice Flavorings

Bonus: Cherry Buttercream frosting

# Introduction

I am a single work at home mom with six kids. I run the <u>Pam's Pride Recommendations</u> blog for Budget Friendly Kindle Downloads for homesteaders, preppers, and do-it-yourselfers at Pamspriderecommendations.com. I do a lot of canning to make my family budget stretch as far as I can. I also have a decent garden that I expand every year or so. These are recipes my family uses regularly and enjoy so I thought I would share them with all of you along with some photos of our canning adventures.

My children and I love pancakes, waffles, and French Toast! We may or may not have several different waffle makers! A Scooby Doo, Heart Shaped, Princess, 4 square, 2 square, and Belgium waffle makers being amongst the favorites with the Waffle Stick Maker being the wee ones absolute favorite! Homemade pancake and waffle mix is so much cheaper than a box of cereal and goes a lot further than a box of cereal does in my house.

We also love cakes and quick breads. Cake mix is one of those desserts that feed a lot of people for very little money. We love homemade frostings and syrups and sauces on our cakes and breads. We also like to have different flavors depending on the seasons. For example we like the citrusy syrups in the spring and the cranberry and caramel syrups in the fall and winter. We do eat most of them all year long though.

Since I have so many people to please I make my syrups with different consistencies too and depending on how we want to use the syrup. I like the thinner syrups for dipping and the chunkier syrups for over cakes and what I would consider regular syrup for ice cream topping and pancakes. If you like thinner syrups use the fruit juice for making your syrup. If you want regular syrup strain some of the fruit out. If you like chunky syrup leave the crushed fruit pieces in your syrup. The thickness of the syrup will also depend on the fruit that you are using. Some fruits contain more pectin and will naturally result in a thicker syrup.

That is the joy of canning…you can make whatever flavor and consistency you and your family likes best and everyone can have their favorite!

I like to pull out my recipes and can several kinds of syrups in one day depending on how much I have of each fruit and what is in season. Since most of these recipes are made in small two to four cup batches it makes it easier to have all of my jars out and sterile at one time and process one batch after another. I also like to use what we call 'cupcake' size canning jars. They are the 4 oz. Ball canning jars. Then I use my Tattler Reusable canning lids so they are canned in easy single serve size and everyone can pull out the flavor they like best. Some syrups the whole family loves so I can those in pint size jars.

# How to Can Syrup

Bring water to boil in a large pot and carefully place in the appropriate amount of 4 ounce, 8 ounce Jelly jars, or pint jars for the amount of syrup you are processing along with the corresponding lids and rings to simmer for at least 10 minutes to sterilize and to soften the rubber on the lids. Do not over boil the lids as this may compromise the rubber flange and cause the lid to not seal properly.

Bring syrup to a boil and simmer for at least 5 minutes. Remove jars with tongs one at a time, emptying the water out, and place a canning funnel on top, then use a ladle and fill the jars to within ¼ inch head space. Wipe the rims clean of any spilled syrup. Then affix the lid and ring. Turn the bands to fingertip tight, screwing the rings on too tight can compromise the seal.

Put the jars in the pot fitted with a rack insert and add enough water to cover by 2 inches. Bring to a boil over high heat and boil briskly for 10 minutes.

Transfer the jars to a rack and allow them to cool for 12 to 24 hours. You should hear a popping sound as the vacuum seals to the lid to the jar. When the jars and syrup are completely cool check the seals by pressing on the lids. If the lid bounces when you press on it the lid did not seal properly. You can either use a new lid and repeat the canning process or refrigerate the syrup and use within two weeks.

You can also remove the bands and try to pick up the jars by holding onto the rim of the lids if the lids are tight the seal is good.

I keep bands on my jars only when I plan on transporting them or giving them as gifts. I generally do not store my filled and sealed jars with rings because it always me to immediately see if any jars have come unsealed will sitting on the shelf and so I can reuse my rings on other jars when I am canning.

Be sure to label each jar with date it was canned and the type of syrup. This is especially helpful when you have canned multiple flavors of syrup as blueberry, lemon blueberry, elderberry, and black raspberry can all look alike once sealed and sitting on the shelf.

Store the filled and properly sealed jars in a cool dark place for up to a year. Once a jar is opened refrigerate the syrup for up to 2 weeks.

Because fruits have a high-acid content they can be water bath canned. Acid kills bacteria. Foods with lots of acid in them don't require much heat to successfully kill all of the bacteria in them. Boiling and then processing the jars for 10 to 20 minutes will usually take of the bacteria.

Always consult the Ball Blue Book of canning instructions and follow the proper safety procedures canning fruits and syrups.

## Selecting the Fruit

You should always choose ripe fruit that is at peak quality for fresh eating. Many fruits can be bought year-round at the grocery store because of course it is ideal to use fruit that is in season. Slightly over ripe fruit can be used as well but be sure to inspect the fruit for any mold or off smell and discard it.

Frozen fruits can be used as well and will give you a satisfactory finished product. When using frozen fruit allow the fruit to thaw until it can mash or crush easily. If you want whole berries in your finished syrup do not allow it to thaw completely; just let it thaw until the fruit can be separated into pieces or chunks. This will help them to stay firm during the canning process.

# Apple Cider Syrup

½ Cup Sugar

4 teaspoons cornstarch

½ teaspoon ground cinnamon

1 Cup apple cider or apple juice

1 tablespoon lemon juice

2 tablespoons butter

In a small sauce pan stir together the sugar, cornstarch and cinnamon.  Then stir in the apple cider and lemon juice.  Stir and heat the mixture over medium heat till the mixture is thickened and bubbly.  Then cook for 2 minutes more.  Remove from heat and stir in the butter till melted.  Makes about 1 1/3 cup. Ladle hot syrup into hot sterile jars and process.

Home canned apple cider that we made by putting apples through the juicer.

# Apple Cinnamon Syrup

3 medium apples, peeled and thinly sliced

½ cup packed brown sugar

1/3 cup water

2 tablespoons butter

1 teaspoon cornstarch

½ teaspoon ground cinnamon

In a saucepan over medium heat bring the brown sugar, water, butter, cornstarch and cinnamon to a boil. Boil for 2 minutes until thick. Reduce heat to medium. Add apples and cook for 10-12 minutes or until apples are tender. Makes about 2 cups. Ladle hot syrup into hot sterile jars and process.

This is really good over oatmeal or granola.

# Apple Juice Cinnamon Syrup

6 cups Apple Juice

3 cinnamon sticks, broken up

5 cups sugar

4 cups water

3 cups corn syrup

Combine apple juice and cinnamon sticks in a large saucepan. Simmer 5 minutes and set aside. Then combine the sugar and water in a medium saucepan. Bring to a boil. Add apple juice and corn syrup to the sugar syrup. Boil for 5 minutes. Remove the cinnamon sticks. Stir in the lemon juice. Makes approximately 12 cups. Ladle hot syrup into hot sterile jars and process.

I like to brown and crumble sausage or bacon and put that in my pancakes as I make them and then pour the warmed apple syrup over my pancakes.

Apple Walnut Caramel Syrup

2 medium cooking apples

4 tablespoons butter

1 teaspoon cinnamon

¼ teaspoon nutmeg

1/8 teaspoon ground cloves

2/3 cup brown sugar

1 ½-2 teaspoons cornstarch (add more or less depending on how thick or thin you like your syrup)

1 cup water

1/3 cup walnut pieces

Peel, core, and thinly slice the apples. In a large saucepan melt the butter over medium heat.  Stir in the spices and brown sugar all at once.  Mix the cornstarch into the one cup of water until it is dissolved and immediately add the water and mix and then stir until the sugar is dissolved.  Add the apples and cook over medium heat, stirring frequently, until the apples are almost tender and the syrup is bubbly. Ladle hot syrup into hot sterile jars and process.

## Blackberry Syrup

6 cups blackberry puree

10 cups sugar

¼ cup lemon juice

On the day before making the syrup process the fresh blackberries through a berry screen or sieve to make the required 6 cups of seed free puree.  Store the puree in the refrigerator overnight in a tall container.  I use half gallon canning jars.  Some of the suspended solids will settle overnight.  Gently pour the container to avoid stirring up the settled pulp.  In a large pot add the blackberry puree, sugar,  and lemon juice.  Stir constantly over medium heat until the mixture boils.  Reduce heat and simmer, while continuing to stir, for an additional 5 minutes.  Remove from heat and carefully skim any film that forms on the surface.  Return to heat and simmer than ladle into hot sterile jars and then process.

Blackberry Blueberry Maple Vanilla Syrup

1 cup blackberries

1 cup blueberries

1 cup maple syrup

1 vanilla bean or 1 teaspoon vanilla

Combine fruit and syrup in a small bowl.  Use the back of a spoon and press the berries just until they start to break apart.  This is where taste preference comes in…you can press the syrup through a sieve if you want a smoother syrup or mash the berries sparingly for a thicker syrup. Open, scrape out, and add vanilla bean or liquid vanilla.  Bring to a boil and stir constantly.  Ladle hot syrup into hot sterile jars and process.

## Blackberry Thyme Syrup

3 cups blackberries

1 ½ cups sugar

¼ cup water

3 sprigs fresh Thyme

In a medium sauce pan crush the berries with a potato masher. Add the water and thyme and bring to a boil over medium-high heat, reduce heat to medium low and simmer until the berries are very soft and juicy. Approximately 5 mintues.

Set a fine sieve over a bowl and pour the berry pulp into the sieve and allow the juice to drip through. Gently press the pulp with a rubber spatula to extract as much juice as possible but don't press so hard that you force the pulp through.

Measure the juice and then pour it into a clean sauce pan. For every ¼ cup of juice add ¼ cup of sugar. Bring to a boil over medium heat and continue stirring to dissolve the sugar. Reduce the heat to low and simmer until syrup starts to thicken but is still runny, about one minute. Skim the foam with a spoon. Ladle hot syrup into hot sterile jars and process.

Blueberry Syrup

3 cups blueberries

1 ½ cups sugar

¼ cup water

In a medium sauce pan crush the berries with a potato masher. Add the water and bring to a boil over medium-high heat, reduce heat to medium low and simmer until the berries are very soft and juicy. Approximately 5 mintues.

Set a fine sieve over a bowl and pour the berry pulp into the sieve and allow the juice to drip through. Gently press the pulp with a rubber spatula to extract as much juice as possible but don't press so hard that you force the pulp through.

Measure the juice and then pour it into a clean sauce pan. For every ¼ cup of juice add ¼ cup of sugar. Bring to a boil over medium heat and continue stirring to dissolve the sugar. Reduce the heat to low and simmer until syrup starts to thicken but is still runny, about one minute. Skim the foam with a spoon. Ladle hot syrup into hot sterile jars and process.

Blueberry Maple Syrup

2 cup blueberries

1 cup maple syrup

Combine fruit and syrup in a small bowl.  Use the back of a spoon and press the berries just until they start to break apart.  This is where taste preference comes in…you can press the syrup through a sieve if you want a smoother syrup or mash the berries sparingly for a thicker syrup.  Bring to a boil and stir constantly.  Ladle hot syrup into hot sterile jars and process.

With this syrup you can use your taste preference and add more blueberries and more or less maple syrup.

## Blueberry Maple Vanilla

2 cup blueberries

1 cup maple syrup

1 vanilla bean or 1 teaspoon vanilla

Combine fruit and syrup in a small bowl.  Use the back of a spoon and press the berries just until they start to break apart.  This is where taste preference comes in…you can press the syrup through a sieve if you want a smoother syrup or mash the berries sparingly for a thicker syrup.  Open, scrape out, and add vanilla bean or liquid vanilla.  Bring to a boil and stir constantly.  Ladle hot syrup into hot sterile jars and process.

We seem to get tons and tons of blueberries every year so we process them in the juicer and then I dehydrate the pulp for adding to other things.

One year the juicer kept clogging up.

So after turning it off for like the 10<sup>th</sup> time to clean out the clog I turn around to find this:

I would suggest that you skip the part where you make a mess when juicing your berries. Making you own homemade syrups and canning is definitely an adventure!

## Caramel Syrup

4 cups brown sugar

1 ½ cups corn syrup

½ lb of salted butter

¾ cup of cold water

10 ounces of sweetened condensed milk

Mix sugar, syrup, and butter over medium heat in a sauce pan.  As soon as it starts to boil stir constantly for eight minutes.  Remove from heat.  Add water in 3 intervals, ¼ cup eat time, be sure to stir it well after each addition.  Add sweetened condensed milk and stir until well blended.  Pour into hot sterilized jars and place lids on.  Store in the refrigerator.

## Cherry Syrup

4 cups Sweetheart cherries (with a slit cut in the side)

2 cups of sugar

1 cup of water

¼ teaspoon of sea salt

Add all of the ingredients into a medium pot. Smash with a potato masher to release some of the cherry juices. Bring to a boil. Simmer on a medium high so that it is bubbling but not boiling. Reduce syrup to about half or until it thickens a bit. It will continue to thicken as it cools. Ladle hot syrup into hot sterile jars and process.

I like to use the cherry syrup to make homemade cherry buttercream frosting. Recipe at the end of this book.

# Cherry Basil Syrup

1 cup water

1/3 cup sugar

20 Basil leaves

6 cups pitted cherries

Add the water and sugar into a medium pot.  Turn the heat to medium and stir until the sugar is dissolved.  Add the basil.  Simmer until the syrup is thickened and has reduced by 2/3.  Discard the basil and let the syrup cool. Then mix the cooled basil syrup with the pitted cherries.  Rebring to a boil and ladle into hot sterile jars and process.

This is good over almond pound cake.

# Chunky Apple Cinnamon Syrup

6 cups apple juice

3 to 4 tart apples peeled and diced

3 teaspoons of cinnamon (or to your taste)

5 cups sugar

4 cups water

3 cups corn syrup

1/4 cup lemon juice

Combine apple juice and cinnamon in a saucepan and bring to a boil and then let set. In another saucepan combine the sugar and water and bring to a boil. Add the cinnamon apple juice and corn syrup fo the sugar syrup. Then add the diced apple chunks. Boil for 5 minutes. Stir in the lemon juice. Ladle the hot syrup into hot sterile jars and then process in for 10 minutes in a water bath canner.

For this recipe you can add more or less cinnamon and make the apple chunks as big or as small as you would like. You can also use cider instead of apple juice for even more flavor.

## Cinnamon Syrup

2 cups water

4 cinnamon sticks

1 1/2 cups sugar

Boil cinnamon sticks in the water for 10 minutes.  Strain out the cinnamon sticks and then add the sugar and bring to a boil until dissolved.

Cranberry Syrup

12 oz. Fresh or Frozen Cranberries

3 cups sugar

4 c. Filtered Water

In a saucepan on medium-high, combine water and cranberries. Cook cranberries until they all pop.

Mash popped cranberries with a slotted spoon and remove from heat. Let stand for 5 minutes.

Put cranberries into blender and blend on high for 1 minute.  Strain syrup through a fine mesh sieve. Put in saucepan and bring back to a boil, add sugar and stir until dissolved, boil 5 minutes. Then ladle into hot sterile jars and process.

Fresh whole cranberries are easily picked up in the fall around Thanksgiving time.

# Cranberry Juice Syrup

2 1/2 cups cranberry juice

1 cup cranberries

3/4 cups light colored corn syrup

1/4 cup sugar

In a medium saucepan combine cranberry juice, cranberries, corn syrup, and sugar. Stir to dissolve sugar. Bring to a rolling boil over medium-high heat. Reduce heat to medium. Boil 30 to 40 minutes or until reduced to 2-1/2 cups. Strain out berries. If you would like a chunkier syrup leave the cranberries in and blend them to the desired consistency that you like. Bring to a boil and ladle into hot sterile jars and process.

Cranberry Orange Syrup

4 cups light corn syrup

1 cup thawed orange juice concentrate

1 cup canned cranberry sauce

Combine corn syrup, orange juice concentrate and sauce in a medium saucepan; bring to a boil. Reduce heat and simmer for 3 minutes without stirring. Watch carefully to prevent syrup from foaming over. Ladle into hot sterile jars to process.

This is a great last minute recipe if you always keep these ingredients in your food storage and freezer. I love this served warm over gingerbread pancakes.

Elderberry Syrup

1 cup fresh elderberries

3 cups water

1 cup honey

optional:

1 teaspoon cinnamon

cloves

ginger

In a saucepan combine elderberries, water, cinnamon, cloves, and ginger and bring to a boil over medium heat. Reduce heat to low and simmer for 30 minutes. Mash the berries to release the juice. Strain the mixture and discard the pulp. Let cool. Stir in honey. Ladle into jars and store in the refrigerator for 2 to 3 months.

I am not crazy about the bitterness of elderberry but my mom loves it so this is usually something I make for her when the elderberries are in season.

Hazelnut Sugar Syrup

1 cup sugar

1/2 cup water

1/2 cup hazelnut liqueur

Heat sugar, water, and liqueur in a medium saucepan until sugar is dissolved completely. Ladle into jars and refrigerate for up to one month.

Honey Cinnamon Syrup

3/4 honey

1/2 cup butter

1/2 teaspoon cinnamon

Heat honey, butter, and cinnamon until all combined and warm.  Serve.

Hot Pepper Peach Syrup

1 cup water

1 cup sugar

2 peaches, peeled, pitted and chopped

1 jalapeno

1 habanero

Cut the jalapeno and habanero and boil them in the water for 5 minutes.  Strain and discard the peppers.

Add sugar to the strained pepper water and stir until dissolved.  Add the peaches and simmer for 25 minutes. Strain the peaches or leave in if you like a thicker syrup.  Ladle into hot sterile jars and process.

This tastes great over a homemade French vanilla ice cream.

Lavender Syrup

cups water

cup sugar

tablespoon dried lavender buds

dd water, sugar, and lavender to a medium saucepan and bring to a boil. Reduce heat and simmer for 15 inutes. Keep it partially covered. Strain. Then add to jars and store in refrigerator for up to one week.

his is especially good over pound cake.

Lemon Syrup

12 Fresh Lemons

6 quarts Water

6 pounds Sugar

Grate and save the yellow rind portion from 6 lemons.  Extract and strain juice from 12 lemons.  Boil sugar, water, and grated lemon rind together for 15 minutes. Strain.  Add lemon juice. Heat to boiling.  Pour into half pint canning jars.  Process in water bath for 10 minutes.

Can be diluted with water and served over ice, as a sweetener for cocktails or mixed in with icing for cakes.

# Lemon Blueberry Syrup

cups fresh blueberries

/4 cup water

1/2 cup sugar

/2 teaspoon finely grated lemon zest

a medium sauce pan crush blueberries. Add water. Bring to a boil over medium-high heat, reduce the heat to edium low, and simmer until the berries are very soft and juicy, about 5 minutes.

et a fine sieve over a bowl. Pour the berry pulp into the sieve and allow the juice to drip through. Gently press the ulp with a rubber spatula to extract as much juice as possible, but don't press so hard that you force the pulp through.

lean the saucepan. Measure the juice and then pour it into the saucepan. For every 1/4 cup juice, add 1/4 cup sugar. ring to a boil over medium heat, stirring to dissolve the sugar. Reduce the heat to low and simmer until the syrup is iscous but still runny, about 1 minute. Stir in lemon zest. Skim the foam with a spoon. Ladle into hot sterile jars and rocess.

Mint Syrup

1/3 cup sugar

1/3 cup water

1/2 packed fresh mint

Bring sugar and water to a boil until the sugar is dissolved.  Let cool.

Bring a small pot of water to a boil.  Add mint and cook until a vibrant green, about 30 seconds.  Remove from
water and transfer to an ice-water bath.  Drain and squeeze off the excess water.  Puree mint and the sugar
syrup in a blender until smooth.  Let stand for 15 minutes.  Strain and discard the solids.  Ladle into jars and
refrigerate.

# Orange Syrup

1/2 cups sugar

cup water

tablespoons lemon juice

/4 cup fresh orange juice

est from 2 large oranges

ring the water, sugar, and zest to a boil, stirring constantly.  Let it boil for about 5 minutes.  Add the lemon nd orange juices.  Bring back to a boil and boil for about 5 more minutes or until the syrup in the desired onsistency.  Ladle into jars and refrigerate.

his is especially good over fruit salad.

Orange Vanilla Syrup

1 cup sugar

Zest and Juice of 1 orange

1 vanilla bean

Place the sugar, water, zest, juice, and vanilla bean in a small pan and stir to dissolve the sugar. Then bring to a boil. Turn the heat to low and simmer for about 15 minutes to thicken.  Ladle into jars and refrigerate.

This is really good for marinating fresh strawberries for about 15 minutes and serving over shortcakes.

# Peach Syrup

pounds of fresh or frozen peaches

cups water

4 cup sugar

8 teaspoon ground cinnamon (optional)

tablespoon corn starch

tablespoons cold water

a large saucepan combine the peaches, water, sugar and cinnamon.  Bring to a boil.  Reduce heat
and simmer uncovered for 20 minutes. Mashing the peaches to give it the desired consistency that
ou like.

ombine the cornstarch and cold water until smooth; gradually add to the peach mixture. Bring to a boil;
ook and stir for 2 minutes or until thickened.  Ladle into hot sterile jars and process.

prefer to use clear jel when canning instead of cornstarch.

Peach Basil Syrup

1 cup water

20 bail leaves

2 pounds peaches

3/4 cup sugar

Add the water and sugar into a medium pot.  Turn the heat to medium and stir until the sugar is dissolved.  Add the basil.  Simmer until the syrup is thickened and has reduced by 2/3.  Discard the basil and let the syrup cool.  Then mix the cooled basil syrup with peaches.  Bring to a boil.  Mash peaches to desired consistency.  Ladle into hot sterile jars and process.

Peach Vanilla Syrup

cups peaches, puree

cups sugar

tablespoons lemon juice

teaspoons vanilla

ombine peach puree, sugar, and lemon juice in a kettle.  Bring to a boil.  Simmer 5 minutes.  Add vanilla. Ladle
to hot sterile jars with lids and process in a boiling water bath for 20 minutes.

## Pear Vanilla Maple Syrup

2 cups diced pears

1 cup Maple syrup

1 vanilla bean

Dice the pears into bigger or small chunks to get your desired consistency for the syrup. Combine fruit and syrup in a small saucepan. Split vanilla bean, if using, and scrape seeds into mixture or use liquid vanilla. Bring to a boil and stir constantly. Ladle hot syrup into hot sterile jars and process.

## Pineapple Syrup

egg white, slightly beaten

cups water

cups sugar

cups pineapple juice

ombine egg white in sugar with two cups of cold water in a large pot.  Bring the mixture to a boil over
edium-high heat, stirring constantly until the sugar is dissolved and the liquid is clear.  Boil for 10 more
inutes, stirring occassionally.  Add the pineapple juice to the boiling liquid, stir, and bring to a boil again.

:move the pot from the heat and allow the pineapple syrup to cool completely, which will take about 30
inutes.  Skim any film off the top of the syrup using a large spoon.  Transfer the cooled pineapple syrup to jars
ud refrigerate or bring to a boil and ladle into hot sterile jars and process in a boiling water bath for 10
inutes.

his is really good over a fruit salad or mixed with a strawberry drink or banana pancakes!

# Pineapple Rum Ginger Syrup

5 cups water

1 cup sugar

16 (1/8 inch thick) rounds of fresh ginger

2 pineapples (about 3 pounds each), peeled, quartered, lengthwise, and cored, then cut crosswise into 1/4 inch slices.

1/3 cup dark rum (Optional)

Bring water, sugar, and ginger to a boil in a large heavy pot, stirring, until sugar is dissolved. Then boil uncovered for 3 minutes. Remove from heat and let syrup steep, covered, for 10 minutes.

Remove ginger with a slotted spoon and discard. Add pineapple to syrup and simmer, covered, stirring occasionally, until pineapple is translucent, 6 to 8 minutes. Transfer pineapple with slotted spoon to a heatproof bowl, then boil syrup, uncovered until reduced to 2 cups, 10 to 15 minutes. To can, add pineapple back in and bring to a boil. Add rum to syrup and gently boil 1 minute. Ladle into hot sterile jars and process.

Plum Syrup

cups plum juice

2 light Karo syrup

3 cups sugar (depending on how tart or sweet you like it.  I use 2 cups)

aking plum juice:

it plums in half and take out the pit. Then roughly chop and put in a saucepan with water. Fill the saucepan
out halfway with water.  Cook until the plums start to fall apart.  Strain the juice.

a saucepan, mix all the plum juice, Karo, and sugar and bring to a gentle boil.  Stir constantly to make sure
e sugar is dissolved.  Bring to a rolling boil, but keep a close eye on it so it doesn't boil over.  Otherwise it
uld make a super sticky mess.

dle into hot sterile jars and process.

Plum Maple Vanilla Syrup

2 cups diced plums

1 cup Maple syrup

1 vanilla bean

Dice the plums into bigger or small chunks to get your desired consistency for the syrup.  Combine fruit and syrup in a small saucepan.  Split vanilla bean, if using, and scrape seeds into mixture or use liquid vanilla.  Bring to a boil and stir constantly.  Ladle hot syrup into hot sterile jars and process.

## Raspberry Syrup

 cups fresh red raspberries

/2 cup sugar

/4 cup water

 a saucepan combine raspberries, sugar, and water and cook over medium-high heat until the
ixture comes to a boil.  Reduce heat and simmer for 5-8 minutes, stirring frequently to avoid sticking
nd burning. Remove from heat and cool for 15 minutes.  Strain mixture through a fine sieve, pressing
own on the solids with the backside of a spoon to extract liquid.  Or not, depending if you like a
icker syrup.

ring to a boil and ladle into hot sterile jars and process.

Raspberry Blackberry Maple Vanilla Syrup

1 cup raspberries

1 cup blackberries

1 cup Maple syrup

1 vanilla bean

Combine fruit and syrup in a small saucepan.  Split vanilla bean, if using, and scrape seeds into mixture or use liquid vanilla.  Bring to a boil and stir constantly.  Ladle hot syrup into hot sterile jars and process.

# Raspberry Mint Syrup

cups raspberries

½ cups sugar

cup water

sprigs fresh mint

a medium sauce pan crush the berries with a potato masher. Add the water and mint and bring to a boil ver medium-high heat, reduce heat to medium low and simmer until the berries are very soft and juicy. pproximately 5 mintues.

et a fine sieve over a bowl and pour the berry pulp into the sieve and allow the juice to drip through. Gently ress the pulp with a rubber spatula to extract as much juice as possible but don't press so hard that you force e pulp through.

easure the juice and then pour it into a clean sauce pan. For every ¼ cup of juice add ¼ cup of sugar. Bring  a boil over medium heat and continue stirring to dissolve the sugar. Reduce the heat to low and simmer ntil syrup starts to thicken but is still runny, about one minute. Skim the foam with a spoon. Ladle hot syrup to hot sterile jars and process.

# Raspberry Jalapeno Syrup

3 cup raspberries

1 1/2 cup sugar

1 jalapeno, sliced from the stem to the tip

Juice from 1/2 a lemon

Combine raspberries and sugar in a medium bowl. Stir all the sugar into the fruit and mash as you go.

Once the raspberries begin to release juice and the sugar dissolves place the mixture in a medium saucepan and place over high heat. Add the jalapeno.

Bring the mixture to a boil, stirring regularly, until the berries break down and the syrup thickens. When the syrup is the desired thickness add the lemon juice.

Take out the jalapeno. Ladle into hot sterile jars and process.

# Rhubarb Ginger Syrup

cups pink rhubarb, chopped into cubes

inch ginger, sliced

cup sugar

cup water

ut all the ingredients together in a saucepan and let it simmer for about 15-20 minutes until the rhubarb ecomes pulpy and has completely disintegrated. Strain through a sieve. Bring back to a boil and ladle into hot erile jars and process. You can add a slice of ginger to each jar to give it a stronger flavor as it sits if you ould like as well.

o make a rhubarb ginger fizz add 3-4 tablespoons syrup in a glass of ice and pour club soda over it.

ou can also make rhubarb basil syrup by leaving out the ginger and adding chopped basil right before you emove it from the heat. Or you can leave out the ginger and just add vanilla for a more simple rhubarb avored syrup. That is the wonderful thing about home canning, you can make it all your own and to your esired taste.

# Spiced Cherry Syrup

4 cups cherries, pitted

3/4 cup sugar

3/4 cup of water

1/2 cinnamon stick

1/4 teaspoon of almond extract.

1 teaspoon vanilla extract

1 teaspoon of cornstarch

2 teaspoons of water

In a medium saucepan bring 3/4 cup of water and sugar to a boil and let boil for 5 minutes.  Mix in the pitted cherries and cinnamon stick and simmer for 10 minutes.  Add the almond and vanilla extract and simmer for 2 more minutes.

Make a slurry of the cornstarch and 2 teaspoons of water and whisk into the cherry syrup mixture to start the thickening process. Bring the mixture to a boil for one minute and then ladle into hot sterile jars and process.

I prefer to use clear jel when canning instead of cornstarch.

## Strawberry Syrup

pound strawberries, hulled and diced

cup sugar

tablespoons fresh orange juice

1/2 teaspoon finely grated orange zest

a medium saucepan combine all the ingredients and bring to a boil.  Lower the heat and simmer until the strawberries are soft and the syrup is thickened and reduced by 1/3 to 1/2 in volume, about 15 minutes.  Ladle to hot sterile jars and process.

# Strawberry Balsamic Syrup

3 cups strawberries

1 ½ cups sugar

¼ cup water

3/4 teaspoon balsamic vinegar

In a medium sauce pan crush the berries with a potato masher.  Add the water and thyme and bring to a boil over medium-high heat, reduce heat to medium low and simmer until the berries are very soft and juicy.  Approximately 5 mintues.

Set a fine sieve over a bowl and pour the berry pulp into the sieve and allow the juice to drip through.  Gently press the pulp with a rubber spatula to extract as much juice as possible but don't press so hard that you force the pulp through.

Measure the juice and then pour it into a clean sauce pan.  For every ¼ cup of juice add ¼ cup of sugar and 3/4 teaspoon of balsamic vinegar.  Bring to a boil over medium heat and continue stirring to dissolve the sugar.  Reduce the heat to low and simmer until syrup starts to thicken but is still runny, about one minute.  Skim the foam with a spoon.  Ladle hot syrup into hot sterile jars and process.

## Strawberry Rhubarb Syrup

4 cups sliced fresh strawberries

1 cup sliced rhubarb

2/3 cup sugar

1/2 cup orange juice

3 teaspoons cornstarch

1 1/2 teaspoons vanilla

1/4 cup water

Combine sugar, orange juice, water, cornstarch, and vanilla in a large saucepan.  Bring to a boil over medium heat.  Add strawberries and rhubarb, simmer for 5-10 minutes, stirring occasionally until tender.  Mash the strawberries and rhubarb to your desired thickness.  Ladle into hot sterile jars and then process.

You can also add mint to this. I grow my own mint and love the flavor so I add it to a lot of recipes.

## Strawberry Vanilla Peppercorn Syrup

1 pound strawberries, sliced

1 cup water

1 cup sugar

1/4 teaspoon vanilla

3 strips lemon zest

1/2 teaspoon whole black peppercorns, lightly crushed

(You can leave out the peppercorns if you just want strawberry vanilla syrup.)

Combine water, sugar, vanilla, lemon zest and peppercorns and bring to a boil and then simmer for 5 minutes. Add strawberries and bring to a simmer for 5-10 minutes, mashing the strawberries to the desired consistency. Ladle into hot sterile jars and process.

Shaved Ice Flavorings

cup sugar

cup water

packages of your favorite KoolAid flavor drink mix.

a medium saucepan combine sugar and water, bring to a boil stirring occasionally.
dd Kool Aid packet in slowly so it mixes better.
ir and simmer for 1-2 minutes until it all dissolves and is well mixed.
adle into hot sterile jars.
usually put these right into the refrigerator because we use them up so quickly in the summer time.

Cherry, black cherry, and orange are my favorite flavors. The kids love blue raspberry and lemon lime. There are so many Kool Aid flavors to choose from that you will never get bored with these in the summer!

BONUS:

Cherry Buttercream Frosting

4 cups powdered sugar

2 cup butter softened

easpoon vanilla

ablespoons Cherry syrup

hip 3 cups powdered sugar and butter together.  Stir in vanilla and cherry syrup. Beat until smooth and
reading consistency.  Add more sugar or syrup as necessary.

I hope you enjoyed this book and that you check out my website at PamsPrideRecommendations.com for more Budget Friendly Kindle downloads for homesteaders, preppers, and do-it-yourselfers. Also be sure to check out my other book Canning Potatoes and Recipes.

Thank you,
Pam

Made in United States
Orlando, FL
19 March 2023

31179515R00033